✓ T5-AMZ-153

Courageous
Creatures

Dana White

Illustrations by Derrick Williams

1   2   3   4   5   6   7   8   9   10

ISBN 0-8250-4966-5

Copyright © 2004

Walch Publishing

P. O. Box 658 • Portland, Maine 04104-0658

walch.com

Printed in the United States of America

Courageous Creatures

Table of Contents

Courageous Creatures

Introduction

People love to hear amazing stories. That's why people flock to movie theaters to see movies about aliens and monsters. They like to be part of the suspense and action. And why not? The stories we see on the screen are entertaining. They are more exciting than everyday life. Some of the stuff we see in the movies and on television could never happen in real life. Or could it?

Sometimes, astonishing events happen right under our noses. They do not involve aliens or monsters. But sometimes these events are almost as unbelievable. What are these amazing things that take place in our own homes, schools, and hospitals? They

Courageous Creatures

are the heroic actions of animals!

You may wonder how animals can be heroes. The animals described in this book have shown great courage or compassion. They may have risked their own lives to save their human or animal friends. In some cases, they simply showed a deep devotion to the jobs they were trained for. In all cases, the animals improved the lives of those around them.

Can animals be heroes? Well, you be the judge. The following stories about courageous creatures are true. They may even change the way you look at your own pet.

Remember the Oscar-winning movie *Babe?* Babe the pig became a champion sheepdog. Everyone at the sheepherding contest laughed at Farmer Hoggett and Babe. But when Babe won, they cheered. Farmer Hoggett praised Babe. That meant more to this heroic little sheeppig than all the cheers in the world. Babe loved Farmer Hoggett.

Some people say pigs cannot do what Babe did. They say animal brains are tiny. Animals run on instinct. For these people, pigs may mean nothing except bacon. Or maybe spare parts for humans.

What? Spare parts? Yes!

Some people need replacement organs. Pigs' organs are about the same size as human organs. Researchers are trying to learn how to transplant pigs' organs to people. If they can do that, they will make billions of dollars. And many people will live longer.

But other people say animals are more than how we can use them. They say many animals—including pigs—will risk their lives for someone they love. Pigs can be brave and selfless heroes.

Priscilla is one of these heroes. She grew up on a farm in Texas. Some of the pigs from the farm went to a nearby resort. There, they became star swimmers in a water show. They got a lot of attention. Victoria Herberta traveled to the farm from

Houston. She talked with the farmer about his swimming pigs. She brought a pig home with her and named it Priscilla. She was just a baby, a piglet.

Priscilla became like a beloved family dog. Neighborhood kids would call her from the fence, and Priscilla would run to them. Some weekends, Priscilla and Victoria went to a swimming hole. Priscilla like that. She splashed. She swam. She towed people who held onto her harness.

One weekend, a woman said she wanted to swim with Priscilla. That was fine with Priscilla and Victoria. The woman's son went with them to the water. No one noticed

when the little boy
stepped into a
hole and sank.
He came up
thrashing and
screaming.

Priscilla heard the screams. She quickly swam to the drowning child. He grabbed her harness. She pulled him to safety.

A cameraman happened to be there. He snapped photographs of the rescue. Soon people all over the world saw the pictures. Houston proclaimed a "Priscilla the Pig Day." The city gave Priscilla an award for courageous pets. It was the first time a pig had ever won this award. Priscilla was even asked to appear on *The Tonight Show!*

But Priscilla did not appear on television. The airplane ride would have been too difficult for her. And after all, everybody already knew she was a star.

Spammy of Chico, California, became a star too. This pig was being raised for the dinner table. But when she saved her best friend's life, her own life changed.

It started when Spammy joined Spot, a calf, in a pen. Both were only weeks old. They became great friends. Find one, and the other one was sure to be near. Soon they were moved to a shed. They were about two months old. One dry night in May, the shed caught fire. Flames burst from the wood. Firefighters saved what they could, but could not find Spammy and Spot. Everyone thought they were dead.

But then Spammy's owners heard a faint squeal. They followed the sound. Firefighters came with them. There was Spammy! She was scratched. She had burn blisters. And she had soot marks where she had punched a hole in the shed with her rump. She kept squealing until they found Spot, too. The calf had followed her from the burning shed.

Townspeople heard that Spammy would

still end up on the dinner table. They took action. They started the Spammy and Spot Trust Fund. Money from the fund would keep the two friends alive. National newspapers printed the story. More money came in. Now Spammy and Spot will live out their days together.

Then there's Worf, of Scottsdale, Arizona. He came to the Millers when he was three weeks old. The Millers were grieving the loss of another pet pig. Then the potbellied pig rescue service called. A piglet needed a home. The Millers agreed to take him in.

Worf soon made himself loved. He was a gentleman. He used a doggy door to go out. He was polite and quiet. He especially loved Mrs. Miller's mother, Nana. Nana had diabetes. She used a walker or a cane. Nana and Worf spent a lot of time together. Then Mr. Miller was transferred to a new job. It was in another part of the country. The Millers went house-hunting. Worf and Nana waited for them in Scottsdale.

One afternoon a neighbor heard Worf.

He was wailing in the yard. Worf never made loud sounds. Was something wrong? The neighbor phoned. No one answered. She knocked on the door. No answer. She used her emergency key to get in. Nana was slumped in her recliner chair. She was in a diabetic coma. Without Worf's help, Nana would have died.

Without LuLu's help, Jo Ann Altsman would be dead, too. She had a heart attack in her travel trailer while on vacation with her pet pig LuLu. LuLu burst through the doggy door of the travel trailer. She threw herself on her back in front of oncoming traffic. Most drivers just honked and swerved. But one young man followed

LuLu. He called for help when he found Jo Ann. LuLu became a media star, just like Priscilla.

Do animals have feelings? Could your pig or dog or cat save your life? Well, it's happened more than once!

Protective Pets

Some people are afraid of big dogs. But even those people like Lassie. On television, this collie has been protecting

his young master for over sixty years.
Dogs don't live that long. And young
masters grow up. So boy actors were
replaced as years went by. So were the
dogs playing Lassie. One dog retired, and
another one took his place. The current
Lassie is number nine. But each Lassie is
as dedicated as the others. The spirit of
Lassie will live on forever.

The spirit of Celeste will live on, too.
Celeste was a big, burly weimaraner. Late
one night, she barked and barked to wake
up her human, Deanna Dye. Deanna woke
to escape a house on fire. Celeste was not
so lucky. She died in that fire. She was
inducted into the Ohio Animal Hall of

Protective Pets

Fame for her heroism.

Cesar, a three-year-old boxer, also saved his family's life with noise. This time the danger was not snapping, crackling, smoky fire. It was carbon monoxide. This is a deadly gas that is silent and has no odor. The close call happened one winter. An ice storm hit the province of Quebec in Canada. There was no electricity throughout the province. The Lussier family lit a kerosene heater. But the heater was faulty and sent out carbon monoxide fumes. Sometime during the night, Cesar sensed the danger. He howled and nipped at Gisele Lussier's hand. He made her wake up. She was groggy and sick to her stomach. She fumbled for a phone and dialed 911. Help arrived in time.

At the thirty-first annual Purina Animal Heroes Hall of Fame, Gisele spoke. She said, "I thank God for owning Cesar. . . . I love him with all my heart and so do my children and my husband." Cesar cocked his head, listening. The crowd applauded.

Dogs have been called "man's best friend." Few people say that about rats, but the Steich family of Stuttgart, Germany, would. They had a pet rat named Gerd. Gerd had a hideout in a bookcase. Two armed burglars broke into the house one night. Gerd took action. The rat jumped down into the face of one burglar. He landed on all fours and bit with sharp teeth. Then Gerd took care of the second burglar. He jumped on the burglar's foot, ran up his pant leg, and bit. Gerd was a hero. He ended a series of robberies and murders by stopping the burglars.

The Gumbley family of Devon, England, also owe their lives to a rat. Fido, their pet rat, slept on the first floor. His cage was kept unlocked. The family was upstairs in bed one Sunday night. An electric heater set fire to the carpet. The fire spread to some furniture. Fido ran from his cage. But he did not run to safety outdoors. He ran up fifteen stairs to warn his family. To the rat, those stairs must have looked like mountains! He scratched desperately at the door of nine-year-old Megan's room. She woke up and got the family out safely.

Cats have also been known to save lives. High-school student Jose Ybara of Illinois knows this very well. At daybreak one day, Jose suddenly had a seizure. Bart, the family cat, took one look, then took action. She dashed into Jose's mom's room and leapt onto the bed. She licked the woman's eyelids. Cats' tongues are rough. Jose's mom woke up. She took Jose to the hospital in time to save his life. Later, the Illinois government honored Bart for her "ingenuity and persistence."

Bart could see that Jose was in trouble. But research has shown that many animals do not have to "see" trouble. They can sense an epileptic owner's coming seizure. They can tell that a diabetic owner's blood sugar is life-threateningly low. Some of these animals have been trained to warn their people. The people can then get to a safe place. An epileptic, for example, can get to a sofa. That way, he or she can avoid injury from a fall. Diabetics can adjust their insulin levels.

No one knows how animals do this. Researchers call it the "human-animal bond." And researchers know that just being around a pet does good things for people. The pet does not have to be a dog or a cat. Birds and fish have the same relaxing, healthy effect.

The idea of animals helping humans is not new. Many hospitals and nursing homes have pet therapist programs. Some school counselors "hire" their pets to come to work with them. People talk to the visiting animals and pet them. Barriers come down. Pain and fear lessen. It is a win-win situation for both animals and people.

Of course, some animals are better "therapists" than others. Your own pet can be the best therapist there is! Animals do not ask to be loved and understood for the support they give. They just do it. Sometimes they do things we do not understand. Wouldn't it be fun to know what they are really saying when that happens? Has your pet ever tried to "talk" to you?

Ever called someone a "bird brain" when you think that person is dumb? If so, stop and think. Birds are smart. They can be brave heroes.

A pigeon named Cher Ami proved that in World War I (1914–1918). Cher Ami (*share ah-ME*) is French for "dear friend." He served with the Allied forces in France. Trained by the U.S. Army Signal Corps, he was assigned to duty in the Argonne forest.

The Argonne is a rugged and hostile place. Its deep valleys, sheer cliffs, and towering mountains are covered with thick brush. On September 29, 1918, it was even less inviting because it was booby-trapped. But Allied forces had to fight there if they wanted to win the war.

Birds on a Mission

The Allies needed a reliable way to communicate. There were no radio communications then. But telegraphs could get news out and answers back—unless the wires had been cut. If they had, troops relied on runner lines. Runners passed messages from the front line to headquarters like a baton is passed in a relay race. Runners were often killed. Then soldiers turned to the last recourse—carrier pigeons.

This is how it worked: At the front lines, a folded slip of paper with a message was put into a lightweight tube. The tube was attached to a pigeon's leg. The bird flew back to its coop. Wires rigged at the coop sounded a bell or buzzer. A soldier took the message from the tube. He passed the message on by telegraph or human messenger to headquarters. The system was not perfect. A message could get out, but an answer could not come back. But it was all they had.

U.S. foot soldiers, called infantry, were ordered into the Argonne in September 1918. They carried caged pigeons. Winter was coming. But troops followed orders to travel light and lean. They left their winter gear behind. They carried rations, or food, for only a short time. Unfortunately, this last battle of World War I went on a long time. It went on for two long, cold, deadly months.

A battalion in the seventy-seventh Infantry Division took Cher Ami and four other pigeons with them. Charles Whittlesey, a lawyer, commanded the battalion. By early October, the battalion was in serious trouble. It became known as "The Lost Battalion." It was still commanded by Whittlesey. But it was no longer battalion strength. It was a ragtag collection of survivors from many battalions. It was trapped in what had been a fine defensive position before the enemy surrounded it.

There was no food. It was cold. Enemy fire continued to rain down. Shells took out runners and most of the birds. Major Whittlesey sent a message by pigeon asking for artillery support. He and more than 500 men were trapped on the mountainside on October 3.

By the next morning, only a little over 200 men were alive and unwounded. That afternoon American artillery commanders finally began firing hundreds of huge artillery rounds. They meant to help the Lost Battalion. But the big shells dropped on top of Whittlesey and his men. This "friendly fire" was lethal. And there was only one pigeon left—Cher Ami.

Major Whittlesey wrote a message: "We are along the road parallel to 276.4. Our own artillery is dropping a barrage directly on us. For heaven's sake, stop it." The tube with the note inside was strapped to Cher Ami's left leg. He was released into the air.

Now, only a very stupid enemy does not try to shoot a messenger pigeon. The American soldiers watched Cher Ami rise from the brush. For long minutes, enemy bullets flew past the bird like hail. The infantrymen knew that if a bullet hit Cher Ami, they would die. They were elated when Cher Ami spread his wings. They watched the little bird climb above the range of enemy guns.

The infantrymen did not know if Cher Ami would make it. But he flew twenty-five miles in only twenty-five minutes to deliver his message. The "friendly" shelling stopped. More than 200 American lives were saved.

Cher Ami was not so lucky. Uninjured in twelve missions, he was badly wounded this time. A soldier had answered the bell at Cher Ami's coop. Cher Ami was lying on his back. He was bloody. He had been blinded in one eye. There was a bullet hole the size of a quarter in his breast. His left leg dangled by two tendons. But the message was there. In spite of his injuries, he had accomplished his mission.

Medics worked hard to save Cher Ami. He lived until 1919. He became a symbol of victory to America. He was given many military honors. His

preserved body remains at the
Smithsonian Institution in Washington,
D.C.

Cher Ami was just one of thousands of
pigeons throughout history that served in
wars. Pigeons have proved themselves as
flying heroes. But they are also something
else. They are an historic symbol of peace.
In remote areas, pigeons still carry life-
saving medications.

And at least one pigeon—#167—did
not need to carry anything to deliver its
message of courage and love. In recent
years, a boy, Hugh Bradley, found an
injured pigeon. Hugh nursed the bird back

to health. Then he tagged it #167 and set it free. The next winter, Hugh lay in a hospital 200 miles from home. One snowy night, he heard tapping at the window. He asked a nurse to open the window. She did, and a pigeon flew in and landed on Hugh's chest. It was #167!

The next time you hear the phrase "bird brain," remember—being compared to a bird is quite a compliment!

People who love wilderness activities tell this joke about bears: How do you tell the difference between a black bear and a grizzly bear? Climb a tree. A black bear follows you up and eats you. A grizzly bear knocks the tree down, *then* it eats you.

Notice that in both cases, the bear wins. One way wilderness adventurers can better their odds is to take along a brave dog. Such a dog will chase the bear away *before* it eats you.

Queenie is one such dog. She was running in a park in Canada with her human, Bonnie Pankiw. A full-grown black bear suddenly appeared on the trail. It charged at Bonnie. Queenie growled and bit the bear's hind legs. The bear ran off. Bonnie breathed a sigh of relief. She was saved!

But then the bear came back! This time it tried to get around Queenie, a Labrador/German shepherd mix. Again Queenie took action. The bear ran. But it was still not ready to give up. It returned yet again. For the third time Queenie drove it away. The bear finally quit. Bonnie was saved. And Queenie was inducted into the 2002 Purina Animal Hall of Fame for her heroism.

Many campers wear "bear bells" on their backpacks. The bells' sound warns bears of the campers' approach. Calm bears are less likely to charge than surprised bears. Camper Don Mobley went into the woods one day in Alaska. He was not wearing bells. He headed down to the river to gather firewood. Looking up, he saw a grizzly bear cub a short distance away. He knew the sow, or mother bear, would be nearby, but he could not see her.

The next minute, the sow came out of nowhere and charged him. Mobley ran for the river. Now, it is almost impossible to outrun a bear. So the sow gained on Mobley. He thought he was finished. Suddenly Mobley's German shepherd dog, Shadow, burst from the woods. Shadow barked and snapped at the sow. She retreated into the woods with her cub. Shadow gave chase. Minutes later, he came back. He was unhurt except for some raw spots behind his ears.

Mobley does not know if the sow bear clawed or bit Shadow. But he does know his dog saved his life. That night at the campfire, Shadow had his favorite supper. It was pizza and potatoes.

The wilderness is home for wild animals. They will defend their homes and young just as people do. But not all wilderness dangers are animals. Sudden storms or high winds also can be deadly.

Tom Murphy discovered this the hard way. He was boating on the St. Lawrence River. Strong winds and rough water ripped his oars from his hands. His boat bucked and slid. It was completely out of control. Murphy had an out-of-control boat, some rope . . . and his black Labrador retriever, Pat. Would that be enough?

Murphy attached the rope to his boat. Pat jumped into the water and took the rope in his mouth. Would Pat be able to tow the boat through these rough waves to safety? That was asking a lot of a dog!

Pat began to swim. The boat jerked and splashed behind him. For three and a half hours Pat swam. The job seemed impossible. But in the end, he brought the boat to safety. A lot had been asked of him, and Pat had given it. He was later inducted into the Purina Animal Hall of Fame.

Animals help people in other natural disasters, too. In snowy mountains, huge masses of snow can rumble down to bury anything in their path. Avalanche! A person caught in an avalanche is swept helplessly down the mountainside and buried alive. After thirty minutes, that person has only a 50 percent chance to survive. That's where service dogs and their handlers come in. Avalanche rescue dogs are trained to find a person's scent under the snow. They also help dig out trapped people.

Some people say that service dogs help people because of self-interest. They say that a yellow Labrador retriever named Keno saved an avalanche victim only because he knew he would get a reward.

But there are records of wild animals who helped people they did not know. These animals had no hope of reward. There is one story of a wild monkey that helped a soldier during World War II. The soldier had parachuted into Sumatra. His parachute snagged in a tree. He dangled there, helpless. He soon realized he would starve to death if help did not come.

Then a wild monkey showed up. The monkey offered the soldier a banana. The soldier took it. The monkey left . . . and came back with bamboo shoots. The monkey brought food for several days, until the man could finally free himself.

Why did the monkey help the soldier? There was nothing in it for him. No reward, no loving human-animal bond. Could the monkey have fed the man just because the man needed help? But how would the monkey have known that? After all, the monkey lived in trees. Why shouldn't the man live there, too?

Could the man have *told* the monkey somehow?

It sounds strange. But many people have reported communicating with animals in pictures rather than words. They describe instant flashes of feelings. Perhaps this communication goes both ways. That could be how some of these wild animal rescuers like the monkey know when humans need help. Who knows?

9/11/01.
Two planes strike the World Trade Center.

Broadcasters run images of the towers

crumpling and collapsing over and over.
Rescuers arrive to help. They are police,
firefighters, emergency medical units . . .
and dogs. Search and Rescue (SAR) dogs
and their handlers pour into Ground Zero.
They come from across the nation.

It was hot, dusty, lethal work. Shouts
of "Dog over here!" punctuated the eerie
silence. Dogs would sniff out the dying
and the dead. Paul Morgan and his golden
retriever Cody were there. Morgan's
buddy, Hal, and his dog, Sue, were with
them. They took a quick break when the
dogs needed water. Hal found a metal tray
in a trash pile. Morgan's Internet diary
shows how vital and valued these dogs

were: "[O]ut of nowhere a line of firefighters with dirty grim faces passed by, each of them pouring out their own water into the metal tray." And the dogs drank.

Among the 300 dogs at Ground Zero was Servus. He is a seventy-pound Belgian Malinois, nicknamed "Wuss." His partner is Chris Christensen, an Illinois police officer. They were searching a tunnel beneath the Towers. They heard a firefighter bang his ax against a steel beam three times. That meant "Get out! Another building is coming down."

But getting out was impossible.

Christensen and Wuss could not even turn around. Then something gave way. Wuss tumbled headfirst to the bottom of a 20-foot pit. He went into convulsions. Christensen clambered down. Wuss was suffocating. His nose was packed with debris. His tongue was turning purple. Christensen called, "My dog's in trouble!"

Within seconds, firefighter arms reached down. They took Wuss as Christensen passed him up the hole. But Wuss was shaking. Oxygen and an intravenous feed from a nearby fire truck could not stop his shaking.

Two people grabbed a stretcher and

carried Wuss down the street. Others flagged down an ambulance. "Humans only," said the paramedic. The police were angry, but quickly came up with a plan. They loaded Wuss into a cruiser. Three police motorcycles escorted the cruiser three miles to an animal hospital. Their sirens screamed all the way.

Soon Wuss was back on his feet. Christensen rode back to "the pile" with him. He told Wuss to stay in the car. But Wuss jumped out, eager to go back in. The dog refused to stay twice more. So he worked with Christensen sixteen more hours. They worked into the next day. Then Wuss again started choking on inhaled debris. Christensen decided that was enough. He took his dog back home to a hero's welcome.

Going home is not an option for some valiant dogs. Only 180 dogs in the U.S. K-9 war-dog teams came home from the Vietnam conflict. That is 180 dogs out of 4,000. The rest had been loyal scouts, mine sniffers, and sentries. Some were euthanized—"put to sleep." Others were simply abandoned. Some were turned over to the South Vietnamese forces and an unknown fate. The U.S. Department of Defense ruled the dogs had been trained to be violent. They did not want to be responsible for any damage the dogs might do back in the United States.

Steven Janke was only nineteen himself when he met Kobuc. Both served at Cam Rahn Bay in Vietnam. One night Kobuc's sharp German-shepherd nose sensed danger. Enemies were creeping around the base's fuel supply. Kobuc gave the alarm. The enemy was routed after a ninety-minute firefight.

Probably each of the 10,000 dog handlers who served in Vietnam remembers a war dog that saved U.S. lives. "There would be more than 50,000 names on the Vietnam Wall if it were not for the dogs," one said. The wall he is referring to is the Vietnam Memorial in Washington, D. C.

Now there is a war-dog memorial in Riverside, California. Dog handlers and

other people paid for it. No government funds were used. Janke and several thousand others attended its dedication. Chris Raper was in that quiet crowd. He writes on-line that he had all but forgotten the names and faces of the people he served with. But he remembered his dog clearly. Dogs named Duke, Prince, Blackie, Nikki, Zorro, Ranger, King, and Major were alive in the minds of others there.

Many military dogs do important work during peacetime as well. Marine Corps military dogs sniff out explosives and drugs. They serve with many federal offices, including the Secret Service. One of those dogs was eight-year-old Robby. Federal policy to euthanize dogs when they got too old to work was still in effect. But dog handlers began an Internet campaign to change that policy. They wanted to save Robby. A bill was finally introduced into Congress to protect military dogs. The bill said the dogs could be retrained and adopted. The bill was signed into law by President Clinton on November 6, 2000. Sadly, that was too late to save Robby. But it will protect dogs like Crazy Joe.

Crazy Joe works for the federal Homeland Security Department. He is one of their 1,200 detector dogs. These dogs are trained to sniff out drugs, explosives, and chemical weapons. Crazy Joe is a yellow Labrador retriever. He was adopted from an animal shelter. After training, he was assigned to JFK International Airport in New York. He was awarded the prize of top U.S. dog in the 2003 Paws to Recognize program.

In his six-year career, he has uncovered more than $10 million worth of drugs. His biggest bust was a 60-pound stash of cocaine in a suitcase. His handler, Cindy Grob, gave him a nice big steak for that. But first he got the rolled-up towel. "We really go crazy, jumping around, and hooting and hollering, playing tug of war—he loves it," said Grob.

Crazy Joe is lucky. He has a great handler. And he'll have a chance at a great home when he retires.

How heroic can a caged animal be? They cannot get out when a dangerous situation arises. Some once-free zoo animals might not want to help people at all. After all, it was people who put them in cages. And animals with "zoochosis" would probably run from people as fast as they could! A zoo animal with zoochosis paces or bobs its head endlessly. Sometimes it chews on bars and walls. Sometimes it hurts itself.

Binti Jua, a lowland gorilla, did not have zoochosis. She had been born in the Brookfield Zoo in Chicago. When her mother could not feed her, shifts of zookeepers took over. They held her constantly and fed her. She thrived. Keepers named her Binti Jua. That is Swahili for "daughter of sunshine." Six years later, keepers taught her how to take care of the baby she was expecting. They gave her a stuffed animal and showed her how to carry it and nurse it. So Binti Jua was prepared when her daughter, Koola, arrived. She was an excellent mother. She petted and rocked her little one, carrying Koola with her all the time. Zookeepers were proud of Binta Jua. But they had no idea she would become an international hero.

On August 16, 1996, seven-year-old Binta Jua was holding Koola in the zoo's gorilla enclosure. One of the visitors to the zoo that day was a three-year-old boy. He was playing at the barrier of the enclosure and toppled over it. He fell to the concrete floor 18 feet below. He was knocked unconscious. His mother screamed for help.

Help came—from Binti Jua. Still holding Koola, she went to the unconscious boy. Visitors watched fearfully as she lifted the boy's arms as if to make sure he was not broken. Then she gently picked him up. She held him and rocked him soothingly as she went to the door keepers used to enter and leave the enclosure. A larger female gorilla approached. But Binti Jua made a guttural sound that meant "Stay away!" The other gorilla did. Keepers opened the door. They had called paramedics to tend to the boy. Binti Jua tenderly laid him on the floor. Paramedics took him away, and the door was closed. Binti Jua, still holding Koola, went back to her tree. She began caring for her baby again.

The boy recovered quickly. And the world responded to Binti Jua's action. She received letters and gifts from all over the world. The American Legion gave her a medal. *People* magazine named her one of the "25 Most Intriguing People" of 1996. Why? Because "Binti Jua became a rallying symbol of her endangered species—and an example to us all." Binti Jua paid no attention to all this fuss. She did not need fame or rewards. She had Koola.

Some people said Binti Jua was not a hero at all. They say she was just responding to the little boy's big head and eyes. These features call forth nurturing responses in all mammals, they say. But even these people cannot explain why Binti Jua would take the boy to get help from other humans.

Caged Guardians

And what of Tuk, a polar bear at the Stanley Park Zoo in Vancouver, Canada? One day, a young man went to the polar bear pool. He pulled a tiny kitten from his jacket and threw it into the water. Tuk eased up, stretched, then slid into the pool. He emerged carrying the kitten between his front teeth like a mother cat. He swam to the side of the pool and lay down. Holding the kitten between his huge front paws, Tuk gently licked it dry.

Now, a tiny kitten is not much like a polar bear cub. A cub can be a foot long at birth. And the biggest enemies of polar bear cubs are human hunters—and male polar bears. Polar bears are predators.

They are at the top of the food chain in the Far North. So why would Tuk protect the kitten?

Maybe he was simply bored. Polar bears are very smart, and there is not much to do in a typical zoo. The kitten was something new. Or maybe Tuk shared a special bond with the kitten. We'll never know why Tuk decided to rescue that tiny creature.

Captive dolphins also perform heroic deeds. For the past twenty-five years, they have helped people with many kinds of disorders, including autism. Children with autism seem locked in their own private worlds. They may not speak. They often do not respond to anything going on around them. Yet after a three-day therapy session swimming with dolphins, eight-year-old Josh, a boy with autism, spoke his first words.

Other people with diseases ranging from cancer to stuttering say that swimming with dolphins helped them. Scientists have a number of theories about why and how this can happen. Maybe healing happens because of the clicking sounds dolphins make. Or perhaps the dolphins' high-energy fields heal. Maybe the dolphins' permanent "smile" relaxes people enough that they free their own healing or immune systems. Whatever the cause, new technology shows that interacting with dolphins makes people's brains change physically.

Dr. Ludmila Lukina conducted groundbreaking research in 1986 in Ukraine. She and her team retrained dolphins once used to explode war machinery. Could the dolphins help therapists heal people? Many of the more than 1,000 patients in Dr. Lukina's study were recommended to dolphin therapy by their regular doctors. Traditional therapy no longer worked for them. Those in Dr. Lukina's study were able to live better lives. Dolphin-assisted therapy works.

Caged Guardians

That raises other questions. Should animals like dolphins be taken from their homes to help scientists make discoveries? Should animals be taken from their natural homes for any reason? What do you think?